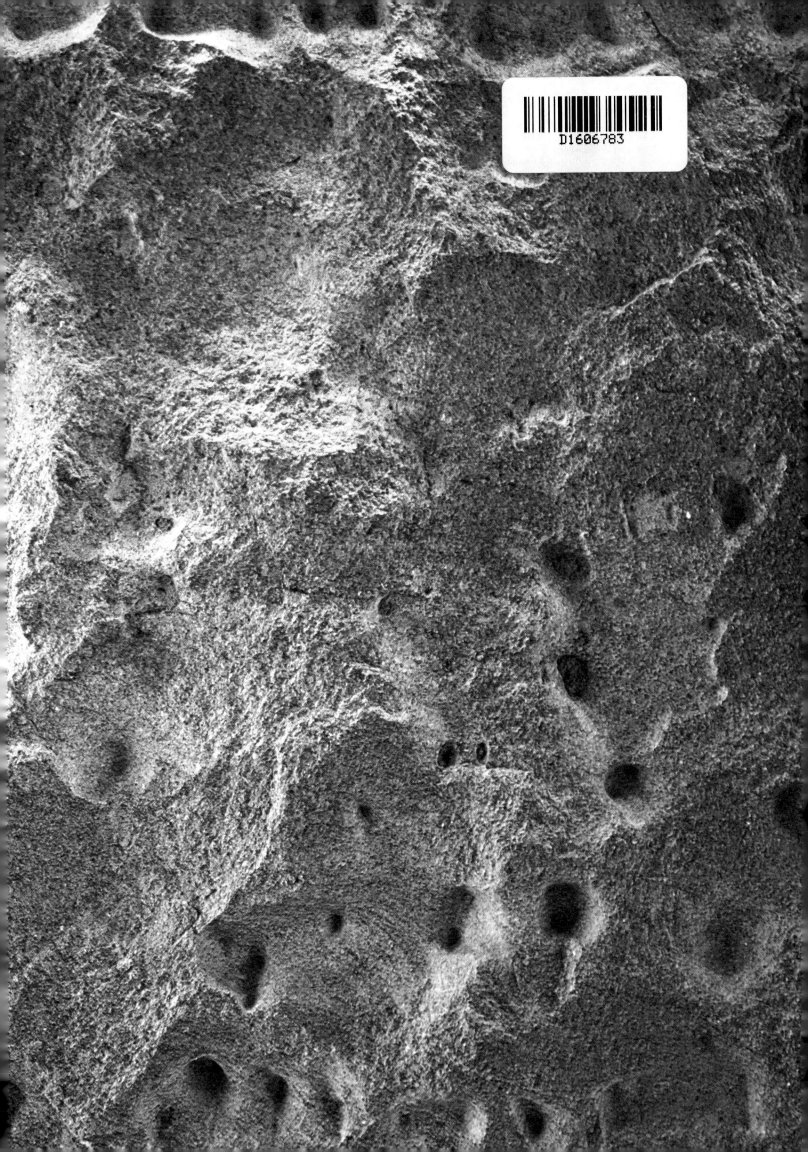

D1606783

WITHDRAWN

Ten by Warren Platner

With a Foreword by Ezra Stoller

McGraw-Hill Book Company, New York

NA 737
.P47
S46

Library of Congress Cataloging in Publication Data
Main entry under title:

Ten by Warren Platner.

1. Platner, Warren, date.
NA737.P47T46   720'.92'4   75-19214
ISBN 0-07-050285-4

Copyright © 1975 by Warren Platner. All rights
reserved. Printed in the United States of America.
No part of this publication may be reproduced,
stored in a retrieval system, or transmitted, in any
form or by any means, electronic, mechanical,
photocopying, recording, or otherwise, without
prior written permission.

1234567890   IP   IP   784321098765

The editor for this book was Jeremy Robinson. It
was set in Sabon by Southern New England
Typographic Service, and was printed by
Intelligencer Printing Company.
An Architectural Record Book.

The completed works shown in this book appear on
the following pages: Kent Memorial Library 6, The
Grill (TWA), 30, Teknor Apex Offices 44, Steelcase
Chicago Showroom 60, Prospect Center Princeton
70, MGIC Headquarters 90, Yale Club 116, Jensen
Design Center 124, American Restaurant 136,
Country Residence 156, and furniture on pages 73,
74, 75, 77, 95, 96, 97, 98, 100, 101, 102, 103, 104,
105, 106, 107, 108, 109, 110, 111, 117, 118, 119,
162, 164, 165, 166, 167, 170, 172, 173, 182, 183,
designed for production.

this book reflects intangibles—atmosphere, light and space, the effects of form and materials, the interaction of nature and man, and the concepts which bind these in physical and psychological reality

369333

Architecture is the framework of man's activities, it contains and enhances them. There is no aspect of this containment which is not the concern of the architect. Vasari wrote that architecture consisted of *commodity, firmness,* and *delight* to which Geoffrey Scott added the term *coherence* as the catalyst which turns it to art.

For *commodity,* read function; for *firmness,* structure (including the proper use of materials); leaving us with *delight* as that intangible, irrational something dependent on but beyond the other two; the responsive spark struck by the individual creative instinct; that most precious and corruptible of our possessions – the free conscience. The three are, of course, inseparable and as a coherent unity they make the art of architecture.

But unity in itself is not enough. It must be subject to the human intellect. The highest unity is in nature – or Nature, as Frank Lloyd Wright spelled it – which is why no design is better than inept design. However the hand of man is everywhere and as our civilization becomes more crowded and the pace of our activities ever more frantic, we move further and further away from nature and must look to sensitive human guidance.

The course and pace of our activities must be reassessed in a context other than that of mere efficiency, whether mechanical or economic. Lately we have been getting a taste of the price of ignoring man and his sensitivities as the module of our planning. In this age of specialization, humane design has eluded the specialist. Of the half dozen noteworthy modern chairs, all were produced by workers in the discipline of architecture where casual concern for structure and frivolous use of materials are not easily rectified mistakes – where the penalty for their indulgence leads to disaster.

We are indebted to the theoreticians of modern architecture for more than just a clean slate; they were not simply architectural nihilists. A new sense of design was evolved based on a reassessment of man's needs in his modern world, discarding out-dated and anachronistic values and their symbols and initiating a conscious cultivation of the sense of logic and beauty that is inherent in structure and materials. But beauty is not simply a by-product of function. Its origin is in the human imagination restricted only by its perception of the problem at hand and its sympathy for the appropriate means for its solution.

This architectural synthesis is expressed to a rare degree in the work of Warren Platner. His analysis and solution shows a sensitivity to our most intimate needs. His appreciation of the *feel* and appropriateness of materials

is supreme. His concern is limit-
less, embracing all aspects of the
project from the physical and intellectual arrangement of the
town in which his building sits to
the landscape of one of its desk
tops.

Every possible element of the
project is subject to his scrutiny.
Every inch is part of the ultimate
solution, coherently related in a
disciplined structure through an
appropriate and exciting use of
materials. The leitmotif of which
we are constantly aware and on
which the whole concept floats is
that superb and unrelenting sense
of quality by which Platner is pos-
sessed.

In most instances the discern-
ing photographer expends a good
deal of effort looking for the
compromise which will yield the
most favorable viewpoint; emphasizing what is successful and
eliminating or subduing what is
not. When confronted with a fine
piece of design the challenge now
becomes one of showing as much
of it as possible, since it is all one
and a coherent statement. Herein
lie the pleasures (and frustrations)
of architectural photography even
more than in documenting the
'great monuments.'

None of the projects in this
book are 'great monuments' in
the accepted sense: no great civic
buildings, no churches, no
museums. Even the library for a
small New England town is a
modest one. Yet they are all important in that they show how the
creative designer can bring us plea-
sure through his handling of the
commonplace. And since the
commonplace is what we spend
most of our lives with, isn't it
perhaps more important to have
these be examples and sources for
architectural satisfaction rather
than just the occasional monument with which we have so little
personal contact?

Moonhole, Bequia
January 26th, 1975

1

On a ridge overlooking the rolling fields of Connecticut Valley tobacco-farming country is the town of Suffield. It is quiet, old and dignified. Walking along Main Street toward the center of the village Green one moves under arching maples past gracious houses from three centuries of agrarian prosperity, houses set in formal white repose on lawns framed with well kept ornamental planting. Passing brick academy buildings and a church worthy of Christopher Wren one comes to the town library in its new structure of white masonry and pink stone. Here the Green sinks down into quiet shade and slips under the building, to emerge inside. Entering through the terraced and brick-paved forecourt, one finds within an order and a character peculiar to this building, to this time and place.

In expressing interest in new buildings in their town, Suffielders often say that they do not care what is built as long as it is "Colonial", a reference to the centuries lining Main Street. The Kent Memorial Library, however, like most buildings, was built to provide usable interior space for a particular purpose. It was, unlike most buildings, conceived from the inside out, the interior in all its aspects taking precedence over the structure and determining it.

In an era when concern for the individual is often lost in the need to plan for mass society, this library has been designed with the conviction that buildings should be built for people. Conceiving of intimately scaled spaces of warm character, like a book-lined room at home, as most pleasurable for the finding and reading of books, the builders have arranged book-walled enclaves of friendly and almost domestic character, of varying size and shape, on five floor levels around a center garden court. Some overlook the landscape of Suffield, some look inward to the glass-walled garden, some have views of both. All have shelving and books as the only wall material and provide for contemplative sitting and reading in a relaxed atmosphere intended to be conspicuously devoid of institutional character. One hardly notices that this library has no *bookstacks,* that one moves easily from one portion of the book collection to another around the garden court without stairs, that the entire arrangement of this building is seen and understood at a glance even though it is made of many relatively small enclosed spaces.

Librarians prefer people entering and leaving to conspicuously pass the charge-out desk. Libraries with small staffs, therefore, usually have but one entrance. Suffield's library faces the town shopping center to the east, an area which provides parking and where shops and services combine in a convenient nucleus of activity. On the West is the town Green and Main Street. Here the slope of the land and the center garden combine so that on this side one enters from the terraced forecourt, passes under the uppermost level of the library, along the garden on brick-paved ramps within the building, to emerge at the same point as when one enters from the east. The internal space of the library thus joins and merges with the public centers of the town.

The discipline and order imposed on the forms of a building by its structure are like the stature of man. There is the frame, there are the many parts supported by that frame and then there are the small details, all functional. On Main Street one is happily impressed with the harmony and antique beauty of Suffield. Built in many styles, set in the green in formal relation to each other, these white and pink buildings are ordered in form and detail once functional but now expressive of a structure no longer used, disciplined by time-honored custom. Products of once-valid technology and discriminating eye, they make the physical reality of the town what it is, collectively they make a style.

Into this and a part of it, then, is a new institution, a building communal to the town, safe, sturdy, efficient, purposeful, hopefully charming. Building late in this century one appropriately uses technology quite different than of the past, not unique to this building but ubiquitous because that is all we can afford. Nevertheless the concrete of its frame can be gracefully ordered, details can be not only functional but right in scale and pretty in the repetition. The structure can be well put together so that forms and spaces are right for *this* building in *this* place and so that details complement the larger sense. Thus on a walk along Main Street one finds this new focal point of the town to be a formal composition of white interconnected pavilions stepping down the slope of lawn, its beginnings clearly defined by a brick-paved base inlaid with planted green, its endings clear in the grey dormer roofs of book-alcove skylights underlined by cornices of overhanging concrete eave. Textures of white-painted brickwork, pink Connecticut stone, yew and pachysandra combine in shade and sunshine with patterns of coffered concrete and metal roof paneling to contrast with leaf and twig of very ordered trees. In intent this entire fabric is the embodiment of the town character, yet presents an architectural order of its own, particular to this building.

The library on the green . . .

. . . surrounds one with books, their beauty as a wall extended into skylit alcoves to make of the entire book collection the internal lining of this building, enveloping the reader.

. . . reveals the many intimately scaled book enclaves at a glance, building and library arrangement easily seen and understood, rising or descending without stairs,

merged with the garden. . . .

Built today, set in New England's past centuries of durable grace, this architecture seeks from its ordinary contemporary technology a rational order in harmony with the old . . .

masonry, glass, landscape and light recombining

n structure, pattern and texture, making its own style.

1

KENT MEMORIAL LIBRARY
Suffield, Connecticut, 1972
Town of Suffield
Warren Platner Associates, Architects
Ezra Stoller, Photographer

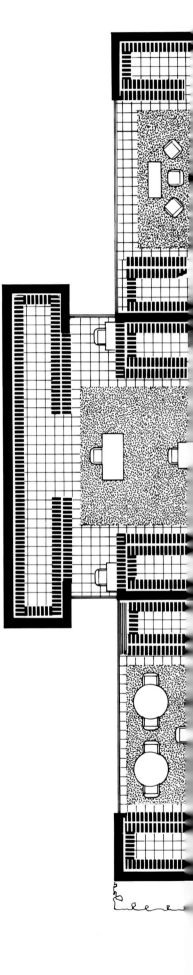

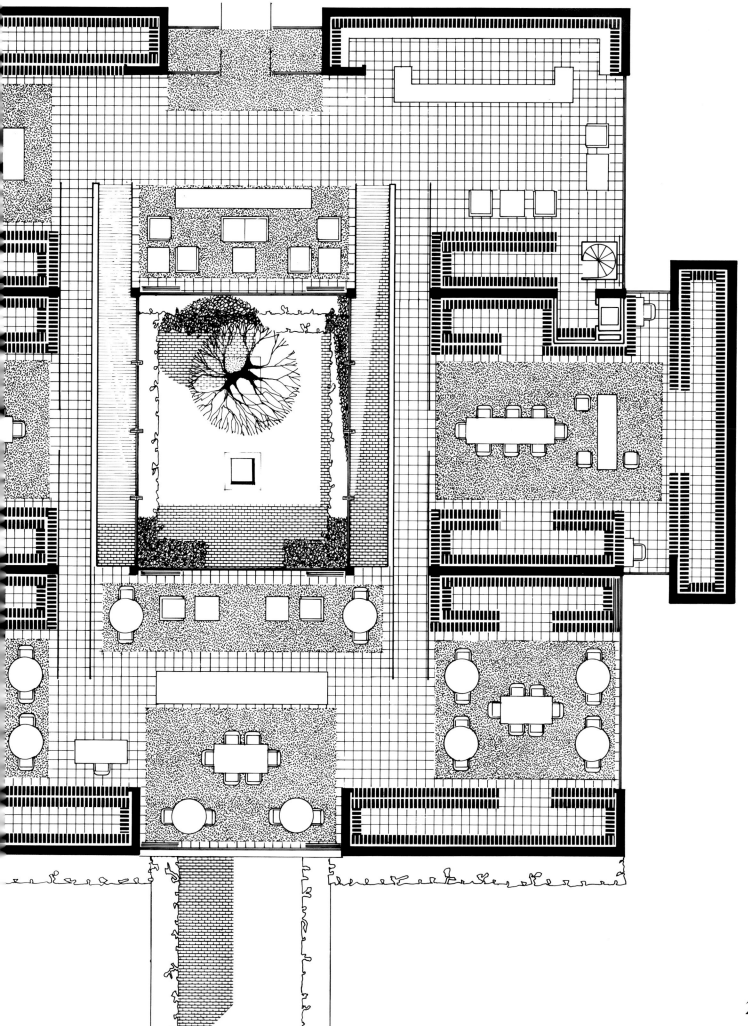

29

2

Air travelers, subject to impersonal system and routine, often find dining in terminal "facilities" as uncharming as meals served on flight trays, especially when these products of corporate imagination rely inappropriately on some reference to another geography, as if the real transposition by air were not tangible enough.

Reasoning that the elements necessary to dining can be in themselves a pleasurable surrounding, the builders of this air terminal restaurant have made of a red, brown and silver design a celebration of the preparation and the presentation of food. Ensconced in leather seats forming the walls and reaching to the ceiling the diner is surrounded by the glitter and color of bottles, reflected and re-reflected in mirrors, reflected again and merged with images of fruits, seafoods, breads, pâtés, meats and other foods. Foods and wines surround and frame the cooks, busy in a fantasy-like hub of reflection and substance, the centerpiece of a dining room where one eats in the kitchen, a commercial kitchen tended by professionals.

The bar is an arc of leather and granite backed by glassware and bottles and their mirrored reflections, flanked by sculptured silk and wool walls repeating bottle forms and ordered into a discipline reminiscent of a baroque façade, textile used as *construction material* not decorative object. Except for these two walls, the whole restaurant was conceived as soft forms of furniture and fixtures, a non-architectural space where the diner would find dining a visual art.

The chef surrounded by the materials of his trade . . .   31

. . . the kitchen and serving equipment, the seats and linen, make festive the occasion of dining, repeating in reflections the images of cooking and eating to emphasize their intrinsic elegance . . .

. . . intensifying the experience of dining itself, massing, multiplying what is most essential and expressive.

Ranked bottles complemented by deep sculptural forms of wool and silk become a structural presence like a baroque façade, the only walls in an architecture devoid of all but visual structure . . .

an architecture of small things in

compartments, of illusory distortions.

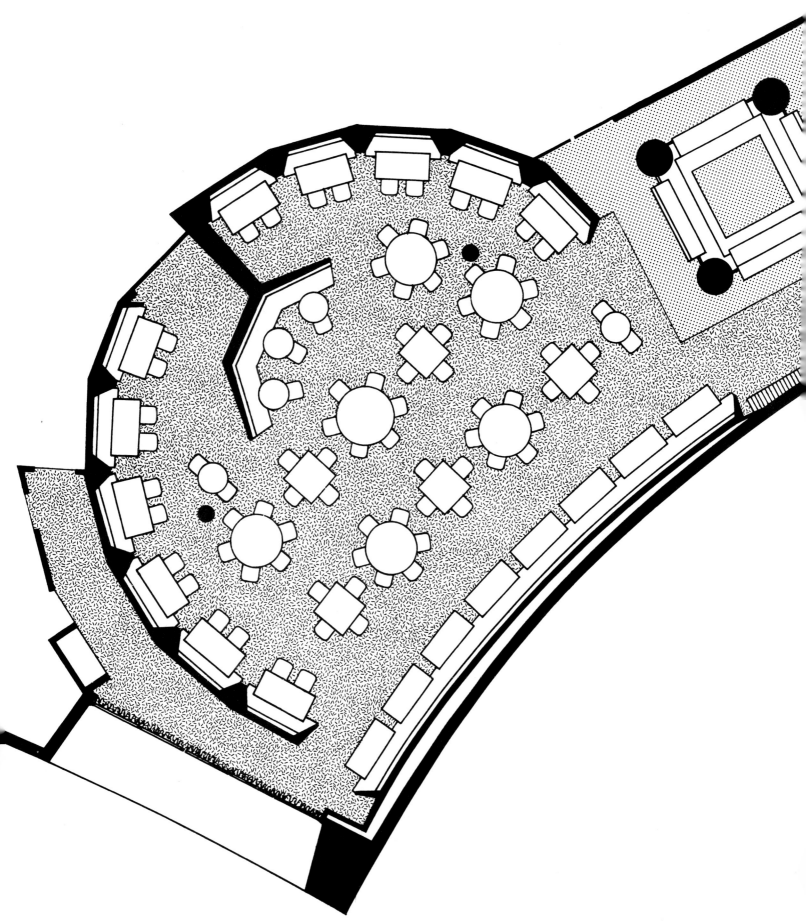

42

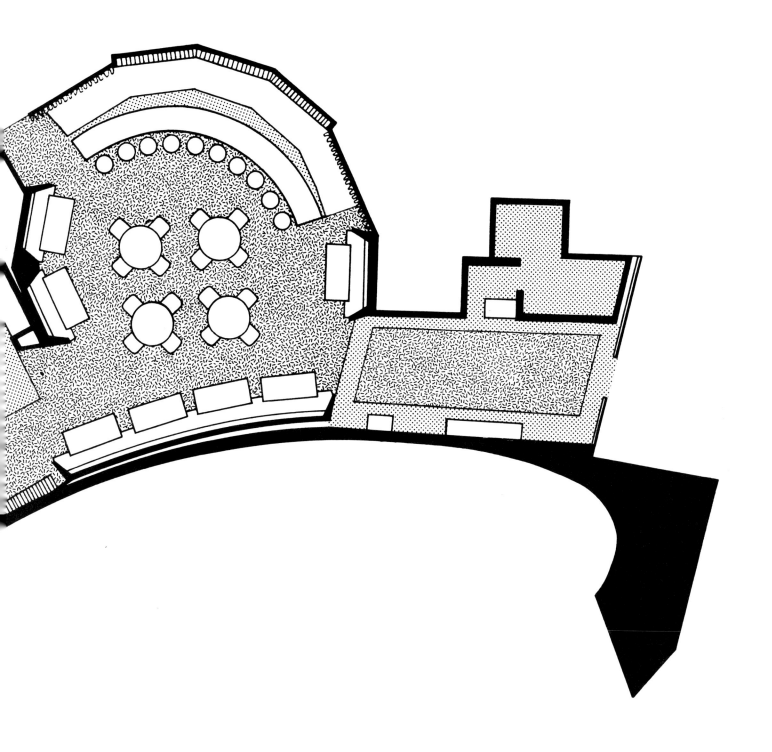

2

THE GRILL
JFK International Airport, 1970
Trans World Airlines
Warren Platner, Architect
(With Kevin Roche, John Dinkeloo and Associates)
Alexandre Georges, Photographer

3

Much of what is old has never been fashionable, only partly successful in an acceptable way and taken for granted when new. This undistinguished past, nevertheless, can serve to enrich the present. One can respond to the crude grace of a façade, to the texture of a style or the flavor of very ordinary but pleasing old forms, as well as to an important historical monument. Moreover, in embracing the ordinary past, one can simply accept what is there, turning attention to values more basic than one style or another.

This renovation of a nineteenth-century industrial complex in a decayed urban area conserves and extends the old, aiming to use it well, adding new construction, transforming space, gaining utility and efficiency – a small renewal avoiding destruction and replacement. Here in a mixed neighborhood of commercial strip, faded houses and industry, the existing factory buildings have been rejuvenated, adjacent once-commercial structures have been put to new use, new construc-

tion has been added for offices and the unused exterior space now serves both occupants and community, all at minimal cost.

In striving to achieve these ends a surprising conception has emerged in the form of regained exterior spaces. Passing by on any of the streets around these old factory buildings we are gently conscious of window and door openings of arched brickwork repeating rhythmically, although sometimes interrupted, in a continuous façade of mellow old masonry. Within we know are the workers and the machines. Extending this masonry wall, the builders have wrapped it around the whole complex, embracing the buildings and exterior space alike. Those spaces themselves become walled gardens which the workers within look out upon and through which the passerby may look or pass. These secluded gardens could have been private but the wide arches return them to the community, thereby also making them more interesting from the interior. Factory workers now enter through the brick-paved tree-shaded garden court, passing under the arches and into the old buildings. This court is also seen from within the offices. Another larger court and its simple but ample planting is reflected and doubled in the mirror-glass window façade of the new building where frugal but pleasant offices overlook this garden through the broad expanse of window. Here also the passerby may look in or walk through from one street to another, the atmosphere of this peaceful court experience in a small way modifying a busy urban day.

The concept is a simple one: the worker is invited to enter, the quiet view from working spaces is a charming relief, the passerby glances in to enjoy the oasis and the whole is accomplished modestly with an indigenous New England mill vocabulary. Thus the result *appears* to be *what* it is *where* it is, and familiar in its Rhode Island locale.

. . . wall wrapping buildings and space again to place these offices on their own park, secluded from commercial strip, not private, open to the community, letting the passerby enjoy the green and its windowed reflections,

letting him stroll through . . .

51

. . . or enter where
garden reflections join
with the interior space.

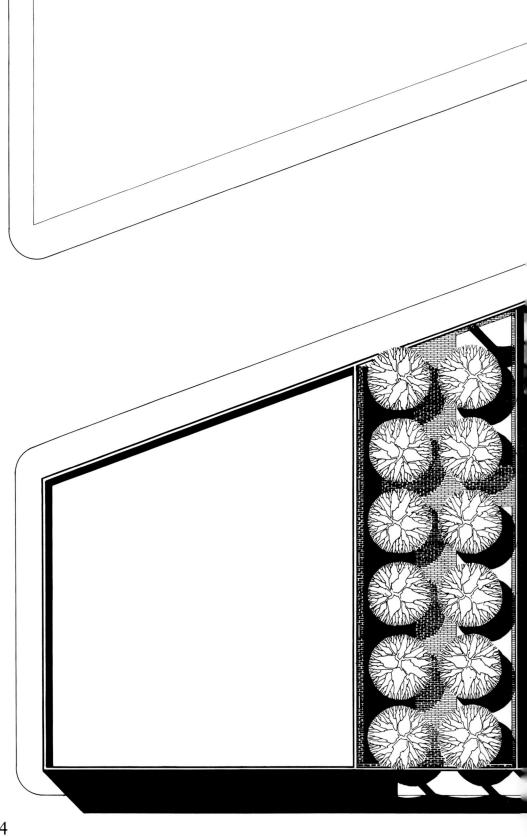

3

HEADQUARTERS OFFICES
Pawtucket, Rhode Island, 1974
Teknor Apex Company
Warren Platner Associates, Architects
Ezra Stoller, Photographer

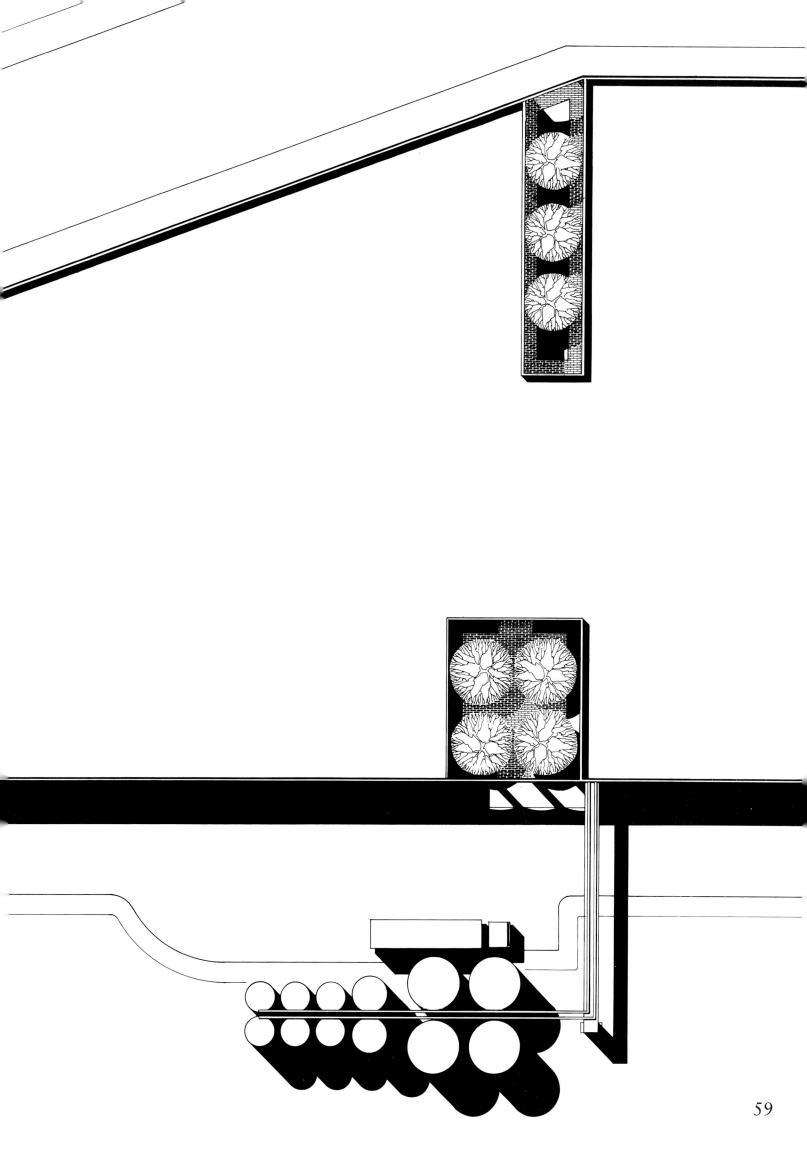

4

To the eye of the beholder, architecture often appears to be created solely for visual effect, that characteristic of it being commonly so emphasized in arbirary assertion. There are, however, occasions when the purpose and intent of building is properly and solely to provide a visual frame of reference, a context for something other than itself, the utility involved being in this framing function. An exhibition can provide a bland characterless space, a void in which to see the exhibited. On the other hand, it can provide a strong and purposeful image, creating a story in depth behind that which is exhibited. Then we have not only the association of image with object, but we have the use of image to imply character.

In this office furniture exhibition in Chicago, it was intended that well made but common products would be not only clearly seen and imbued with the added glamour of their setting, but that, by implication, the whole endeavor behind these products would be colored by the image of the presentation. Here are light and shadow, reflection and transparency, an architecture without substance, the viewer and viewed alike held in a suspension of images in a supporting light-filled atmosphere. The design is made of the products, their reflections and graphic images related to the products. Surfaces are reflective but elusively so. Ceiling and walls are clear glass, reflecting but also transparent, so that what is seen, either through or reflected, changes with the angle of vision, a brilliant, polished surface of crystalline panels reflecting, revealing, elegantly presenting.

The floor is a white mirror, much of it superimposed with elevated sections of polished glass surface. The focal point is the human form, dancing like light through the space, an abstract reference to bodily motion implying that it has been considered. Here the viewer finds a subtle world where even the mundane is glamorous, where all is beautiful by implication.

An exhibition space . . .

. . . in purpose a context for something seen, lends character to things displayed, a suspension of images in a light-filled atmosphere, presenting an abstract image but reassuring in its implications of technical and elegant conformity with the laws of geometry.

A human form, like light dancing through space . . .

62

. . . a respect for bodily
motion, relating man to
useful objects.

Surfaces of clear
glass . . .

65

. . . reflecting, revealing, presenting weightless ethereal images, surfaces themselves hard and palpable, with the solidity, structure, and precision of the furniture that they display.

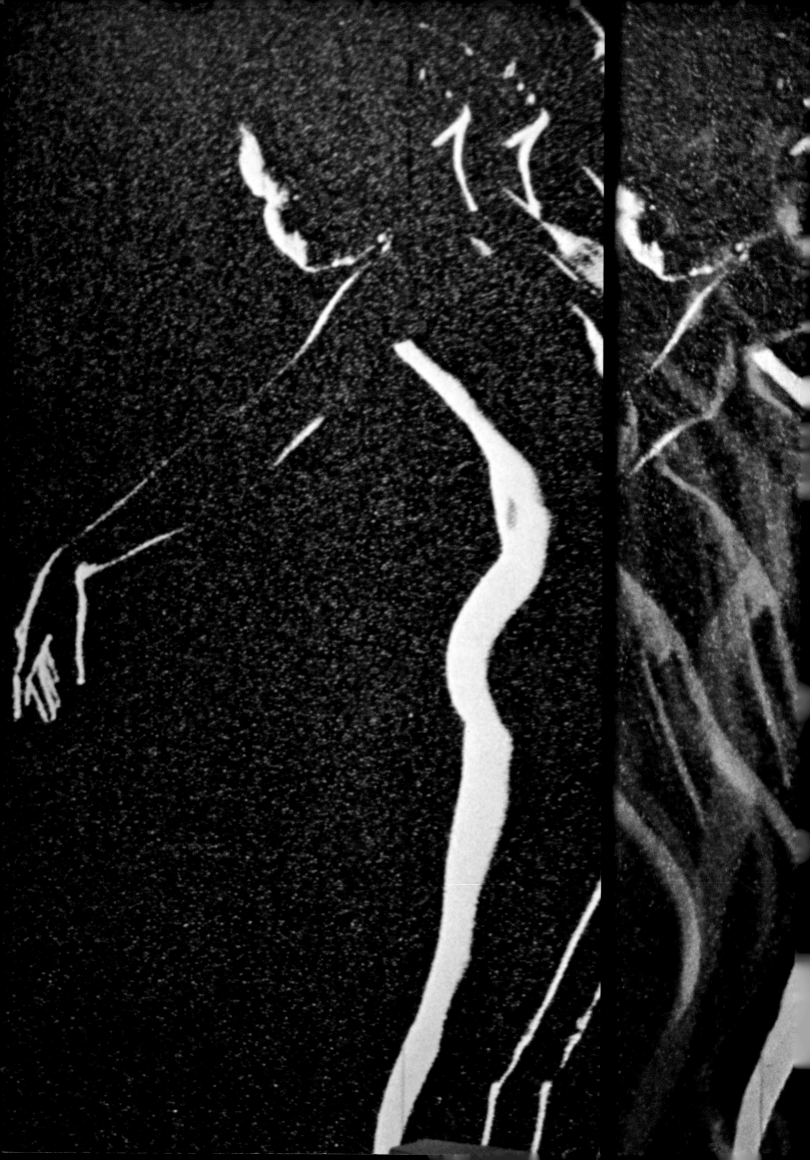

4

SHOWROOM
Chicago, Illinois, 1969
Steelcase, Incorporated
Warren Platner Associates, Architects
Ezra Stoller, Photographer

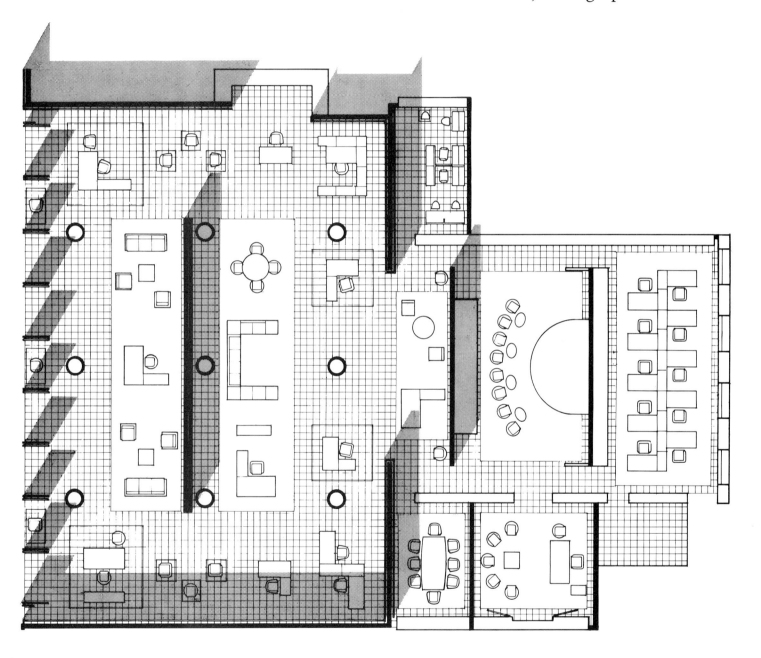

5

The old mansion called Prospect stands at the center of the Princeton campus, secluded behind ancient trees and hedges. Once the residence of university presidents, it is now the Faculty Center, an intellectual and social seat, an institution within an institution. Here this great house continues on, with teaching assistants, deans and solons claiming as theirs a place where once they were but guests. Solidly built (the floor timbers are filled in between with packed clay for mass), this romantic 1849 American version of a Tuscan villa is here to stay, its charming virtues of space and form surviving, serving changed needs and fashions in a changed world. Conversing in or passing through these rooms one is pleased by the fine proportions of established, inwardly-oriented nineteenth-century style, now unified by a lining of airy white and removal of a century's accretion of personal decoration. In the furnishings, contemporary things take their places with the old; form, line and detail joining in character, desires of comfort and institutional life-style accommodated.

Beyond the essentially closed interiors of this substantial edifice is an Italianate garden, a small park semi-circular in shape, walled in privacy by hedge trees and the stonework of the house. Needing large, open dining spaces (the many bedrooms were converted to private conference-dining rooms) for faculty members and their guests, the University has built on this side a glassy dining pavilion which projects into and overlooks the garden. Sitting in this crystalline space, the diner is surrounded by the garden, in fact, *in* it, the forms, textures and details of the planting as much a part of the architecture as concrete, wood and glass. From the garden, the crystal box of the room, set on its recessed hollow pedestal and capped with a wide overhanging masonry roof frankly structural though coffered in the classical way, contrasts with the density of the old edifice, a new element composing with the old.

After dark, the oak louvered sliding sun screens make an enclosing interior lining of delicately scaled wood paneling, lamps at the intersections of the ceiling coffers riding over the diners like a field of stars on a flag.

Once a mansion for the university president,
this great house is now the Faculty Center . . .

. . . a succession of square, broad-roofed forms sheltering inward-looking gracious rooms.

Baroque spaces and classical elements accommodate new uses and contemporary forms, united and articulated by airy white.

. . . walled in privacy by the hedge trees and the stonework of the house, a glass dining pavilion, a new element in composition with the old.

. . . the diner sits on this landscape-surrounded pedestal,

by day a shaded spot in the garden . . .

. . . by night a room turned inward.   After dark sliding louvered panels of oak fill the walls

with a delicate lining of crafted wood, the ceiling changing from shade to source of light.

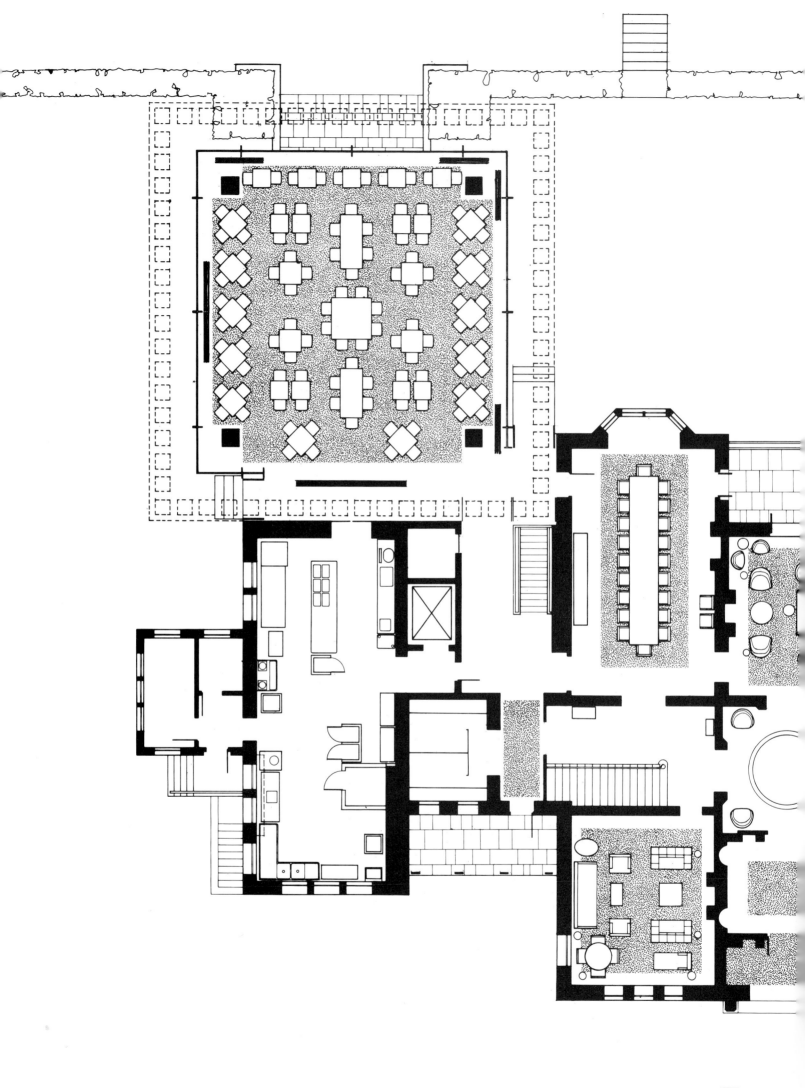

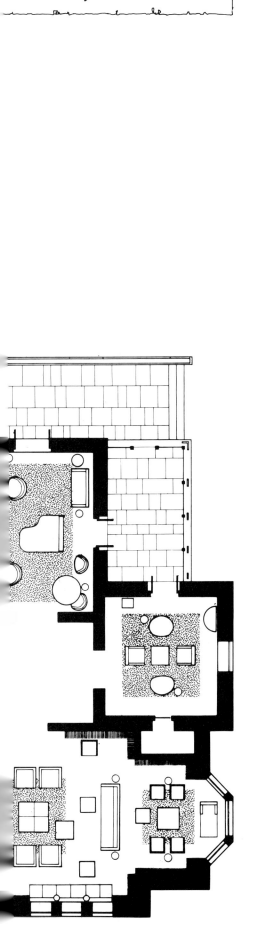

5

PROSPECT CENTER
Princeton, New Jersey, 1970
Princeton University
Pietro Belluschi, Consulting Architect
Warren Platner Associates, Associate Architect
C. Harrison Hill, University Architect
Ezra Stoller, Photographer

6

Offices have been the subject of unending studies involving millions of working people. While there have been continuing attempts, along with the thrust for efficiency, to make *attractive* spaces, the *subject* of offices tends to be one popular only with those who have to provide for them. Psychologically and aesthetically, they have limited appeal. Man's unconscious identification with the character of the spaces he inhabits is generally strong. He likes houses, has an interest in factories—those big machines and spaces he feels are his—even the crowded newsroom of a newspaper has its attraction, like that of the smoke-filled back rooms at a political convention. Offices have very little glamour attached to them because, rightly or wrongly, they are symbols of impersonal system and daily routine, both in the way they are used and how they are put together. In a time of impermanence and change, offices are frequently built in insubstantial character camouflaged with irrelevant decoration of confusing variety. One may occupy an office today and have the uneasy feeling that next week the secretarial pool will have taken it over. And what about the inefficiency of all the recent attempts to put square pegs in triangular holes, visual confusion following on functional waste?

In recognition that office workers spend much of their lives day in and day out in working spaces, these corporate offices for an insurance company were intended to provide both efficient work space and a character responsive to the needs of the individual. Since the individuals form a working community and since they and the company could have in these offices a special character of their own, consistency throughout was an aim. Further, just as much concern was shown for needs and amenities of clerks and typists as for those of corporate officers.

Large spaces not being needed, only spaces of modest dimension were built: here could be no grand spatial effects. Spaces were meticulously fitted into the structural frame, columns, beams, subdividing partitions and furniture working together to create an ordered sequence embracing the various kinds of work at hand. The receptionist and the visitor here find ceremonial spaces appropriate to the occasion, made of the basic structural parts but so arranged as to give this part of the consistent character its clear functional aspect. Offices and conference rooms are intended, clearly, for contemplative, communicative or decisive use, not aspiring to be some other type of space such as an art gallery. The lounges and lunch rooms are intended for just those functions, as a part of these particular buildings, not pretending to be somewhere else and not impersonally devoid of warmth. All these spaces are finite and tangible in form, not vague, sliding space. One feels established and supported psychologically in them. In other words, the thoughtful creation of meaningful physical spaces, in sequence and relation, has been a basic consideration.

Using the two buildings and the logic of providing for the work to be done in them, these spaces derive their character from the necessary elements of architecture and equipment, a consistent vocabulary of form, material, color, light and detail encompassing all parts. An effect of both substance and style comes from the use of the structural concrete panels as a finished ceiling. Many other elements such as room configuration integrate with this ceiling, others such as the use of panelled surfaces relating to it. Partition panelling carefully embraces travertine-covered columns and the textures of rough plaster, enamel, stone, concrete and textile – all in creamy color – work together as one enriched material.

Decorative patterning of surface and material, used in ceremonial spaces for principal walls, is integrated in both design and construction with the architectural elements. The wall in the plaza-level elevator lobby is a block of granite with a trimly bordered field of sculptural rough fractures. The

outer lobby is small and, since one only passes quickly through it, is minimal in design elements. The elevator lobby is also very small but it is also a focal point, a destination, so the emphasis of the granite is reflected in the polished bronze ceiling, walls and doors, increasing both the size and visual importance of this space. On floors above, the lobbies are plain since here again one but passes quickly through.

It is the reception rooms which acquire ceremonial importance, in each the receptionist working at her desk, seen before a textile wall of repetitive large-scale textural pattern, again a wall of sculptural relief and architectural scale but here in silk and linen rather than stone.

In placing these eight focal walls in the buildings, light has played an important role. By using here strong incandescent illumination not only is the sculptural relief shown in dramatic focus, light joining with form, but the life and softness of the incandescent effect is imparted to the people in these spaces in its most effective way. Here because it is the most efficient means of lighting work areas, the fluorescent source has been made a part of the structural ceiling so that it merges with that substantial effect rather than interrupting it.

In the offices, one finds the same basic elements and principles, here the furniture and equipment providing a large part of the character, since they fill the space. Wood, polished metal, leather and plastic laminate present their smooth, rounded forms to the hand and to the eye. Some of the furniture is tall and partially encloses, saving space and office construction, adding a major element of cabinetry, and subdividing the architecture intended to receive this new element. Nearly all of the furniture is made up of interchangeable system components, providing needed office-planning flexibility, but like the building interiors themselves, quietly there, not visually aggressive.

The ceremonial space of corporate office elevator entrances reflected in polished bronze . . .

. . . a bordered block of granite sculptured in rough fractures suggesting a found object. In reception rooms textile walls of silk and linen announce a destination—light and form joining in dramatic focus. . . .

The building's elements form the visual character, an effect of substance and style derived from structural concrete ceiling and paneled partitions embracing travertine columns. Repeated motives set into the single tone of the building's surfaces, textures of plaster, paint, masonry and textile work together as a single material.

... present smooth, rounded forms to eye and hand.

Wickerwork alcoves and vibrant color give a picnic mood to the daily sandwich.

. . . archaic forms entrapped, escaping, the sculpture freeing itself from the wall.

. . . finite and tangible in form, in ordere

equence embrace the various kinds of work . . .

. . . one aesthetic vocabulary
serving the entire building.

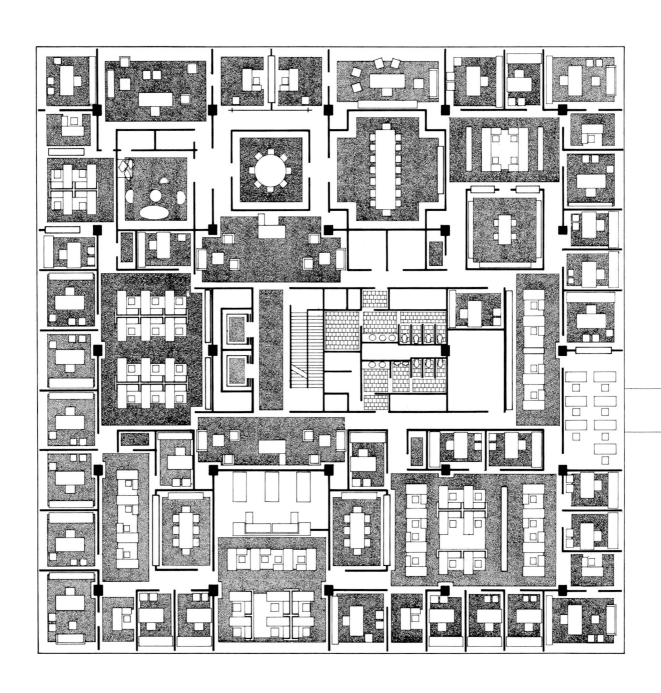

6

MGIC HEADQUARTERS
Milwaukee, Wisconsin, 1973
Mortgage Guarantee Investment Corporation
Warren Platner Associates, Interior Architects
Skidmore, Owings & Merrill, Chicago, Architects of Structures
Ezra Stoller, Photographer

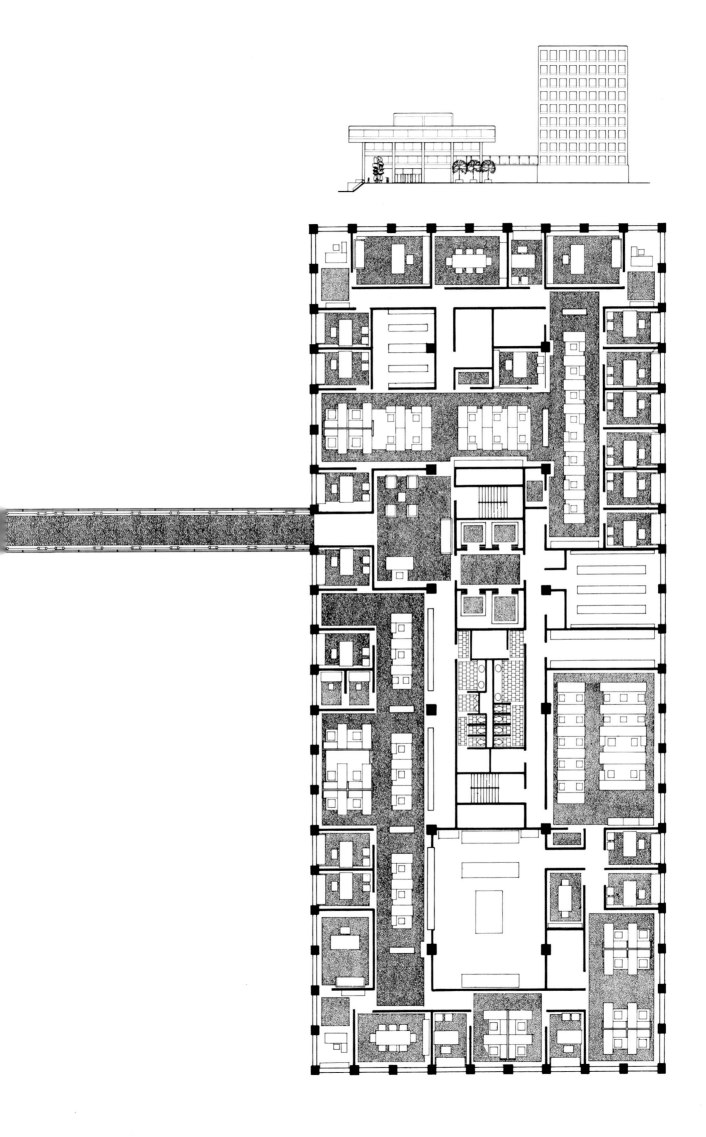

115

7

A member of one of New York's old, urban clubs might well desire no changes, these palaces being built so lavishly as to imply privileged service forever. Needs, however, do change. For instance, the New York Yale Club now numbers women among its members and, while the realities of club operation today dictate economies, the limitations of a building built for unlimited service by unending servants are formidable. So these buildings do change.

In making such functional revisions the Yale Club has set as a goal not only the preserving of old virtues but improving upon them. Thus the intent of this renovation was in part to do what James Gamble Rogers, the architect of this 1914 antique might have envisioned if he could have seen this far into the century. Extending the gracious flavor of conservative old club, the new work is not actually a recreation of old forms, but rather, careful editing and adding of the direct formality needed in this crowded public lobby space. More commodious and economical services, hospitable but monumental furniture, more effective lighting and more manageable and efficient use of space are what the member now finds. What is old and what is new are meant to be indistinguishable, wedded in a single classicism.

Not a recreation of old forms
but careful editing and adding . . .

. . . preserve the
delicately complex
decoration of the old
building, redefining its
clear forms with fine
material and meticulous
detailing.

7

YALE CLUB (Renovations)
New York City, 1972
Yale Club of New York
Warren Platner Associates, Architects
Ezra Stoller, Photographer

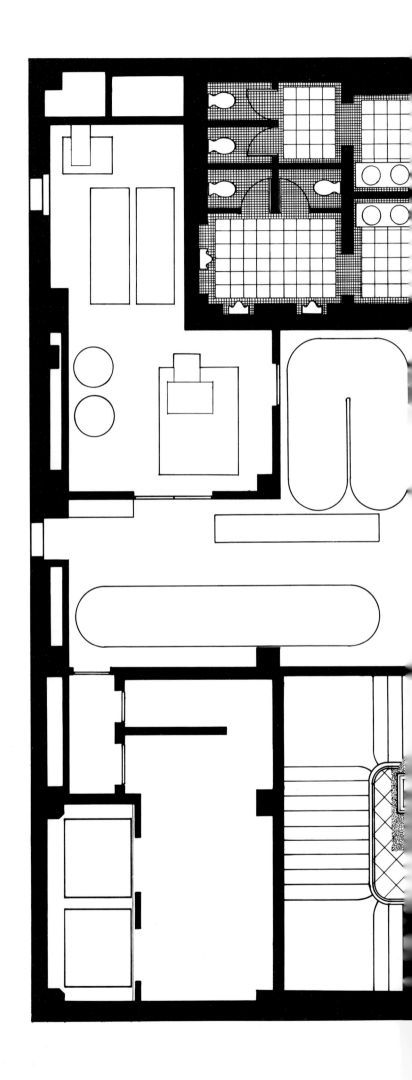

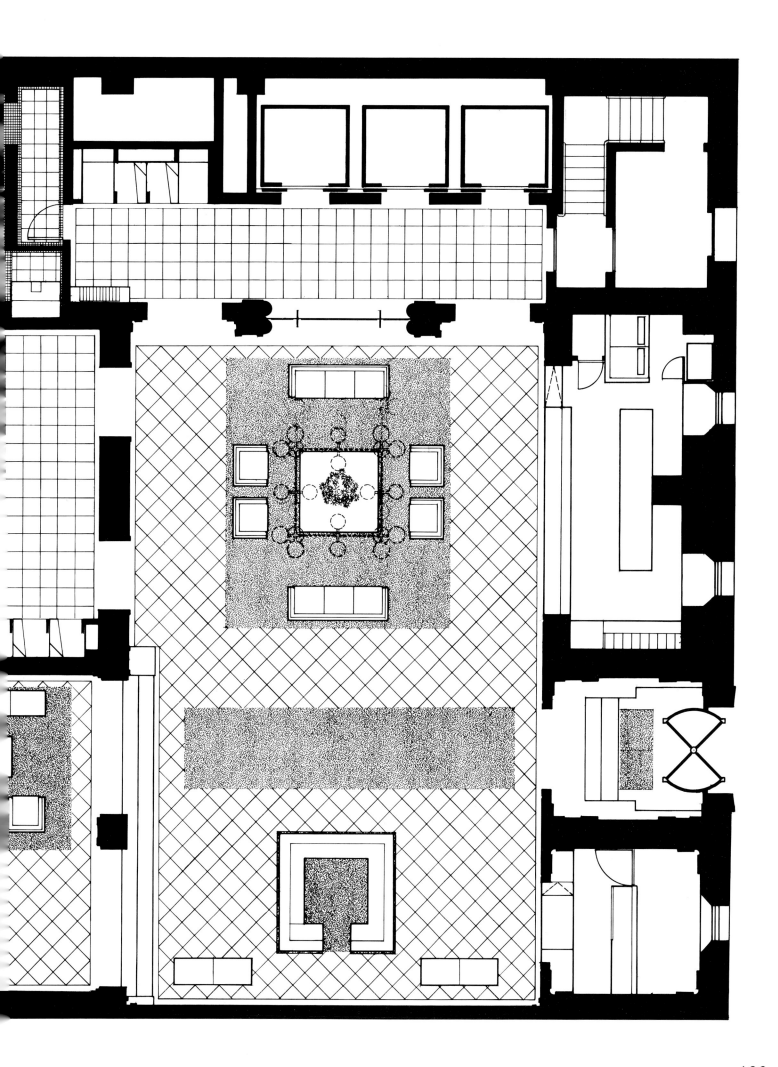

123

8

This Design Center, a large exhibition space in a common loft building, was conceived as an interior shopping street, a commercial galleria through which the browsing visitor passes, past some of the most beautiful objects made. The objects – lighting fixtures, furniture, textiles and small things – are mostly Scandinavian products, many of them of wood. The character of these simple things, good materials forthrightly detailed and elegantly crafted, suggested a supporting atmosphere abstractly reminiscent of primitive monumentality, of bricks, stone and glass, *without* detail if possible. The rough stone floor, whitewashed common brick walls and exposed conduit and ductwork establish this rough but hospitable effect, the architecture proceeding on to explore technologies of glass, textile and light, lending the aura of these themes to the objects displayed.

The transparent, translucent and reflective qualities of glass were here exploited by using this material not as a transparent void but as a space-filling transparent *solid,* without frame, the glass wall *all*-glass, the subtle color of the material imparted to the space. By contrast, textile construction was used to delimit space in deep textural relief, taking its place as part of the architectural frame.

Here, the most important building material however is light. It is used as space-filling atmosphere, as maker of highlight and shadow, it is projected in color images and as showers of shaped luminosity. It is reflected, refracted. It is used to its fullest advantage as both revealer and creator. This galleria has no skylight but one is created of light; there are no trees and no sunshine but leafy shadows and dappled light exist. Objects do not really float supernaturally, but are suspended in light. It is the substance in which people, objects, and structure are supported. These effects are there to look at, but more importantly they were devised to illuminate the scene in a way larger than life.

A shopping street, a walk past beautiful objects . . .   125

. . . where the most important architectural material is light — revealing, creating, changing space to atmosphere,

its energy seeming to support objects . . .   129

. . . showering surface and form with shaped luminosity.

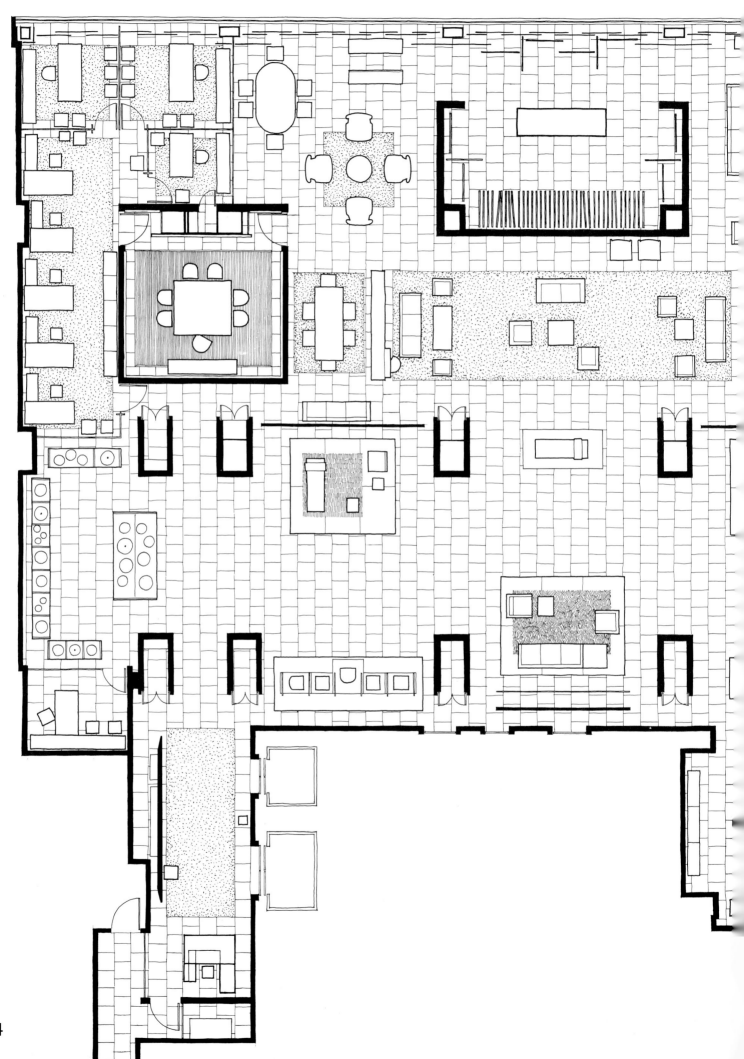

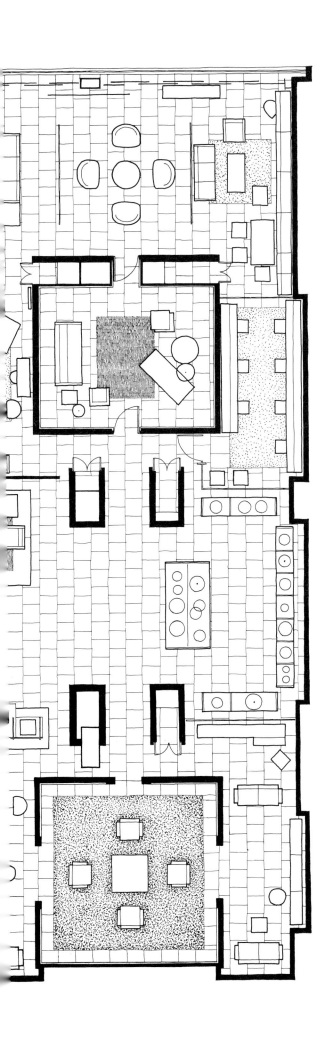

8

DESIGN CENTER
New York City, 1968
Georg Jensen, Incorporated
Warren Platner Associates, Architects
Ezra Stoller, Photographer

9

In a severely plain steel and glass penthouse high above Kansas City, the American Restaurant envelopes diners with its decorative lining, a filigree of wood, brass and lights. Eighty feet square and twenty high, this one great room is by day a luminous, airy volume, with seats in tiers of color ascending terraced levels; by night, a glittering constellation of intimate places, sheltered and contained.

There is an implied contradiction in the builder's desire for elegant popular dining in an impressively grand space, and hence the design addresses itself to the atmosphere of intimate conviviality with which diners would wish to be surrounded. Square canopies of bent wood tracery studded with lights, their four corners descending to the floor, subdivide the larger space, sheltering the diner beneath lacy arcs. The three canopies, really smaller pavilions within the larger pavilion of the penthouse, are similar, although there is a wide divergence of ceiling height due to the terraced floor levels. The arcs of wood are echoed and reflected in brass fixtures hovering like sheltering flowers over tables. Arcs are recalled again in wreath-like sweeps of densely packed loops of white silk and gold on a dark ground, drenched in light so that this wall sculpture seems to be composed of light rather than textile. Exterior walls, all window, are lined with sliding louvered shutters of oak, screening sun and modifying light by day. At night, this shuttered lining sparkles with scattered light, cast like confetti between the warm pools of diffuse illumination, wandering to the tables to recall the festive ceiling.

Bridging the contrast in scale between the great volume of space and the minute detail of food and tableware, between public gathering and personal intimacy, the design entertains the diner and gives distinction to the server in this emporium of elaborate meals.

In the great, luminous glass penthouse . . .

. . . the diner sits sheltered under bentwood canopies whose shapes reappear in lamps like flowers, sheltering again,

in daylight tempered by the shutters' delicate openwork. . . .

A back-bar, with utilitarian simplicity and a brass finish that would be at home on an eighteenth-century naval vessel, overlooks this Missouri meeting place.

. . . sweeps of white silk loops against a dark fabric echo the arc of lights overhead and, as though composed of light themselves, illuminate a more intimate space at evening.

Light, scattered like
confetti from the festive
ceiling, provides a step
between the minute
scale of food and
tableware and the great
volume of the room.

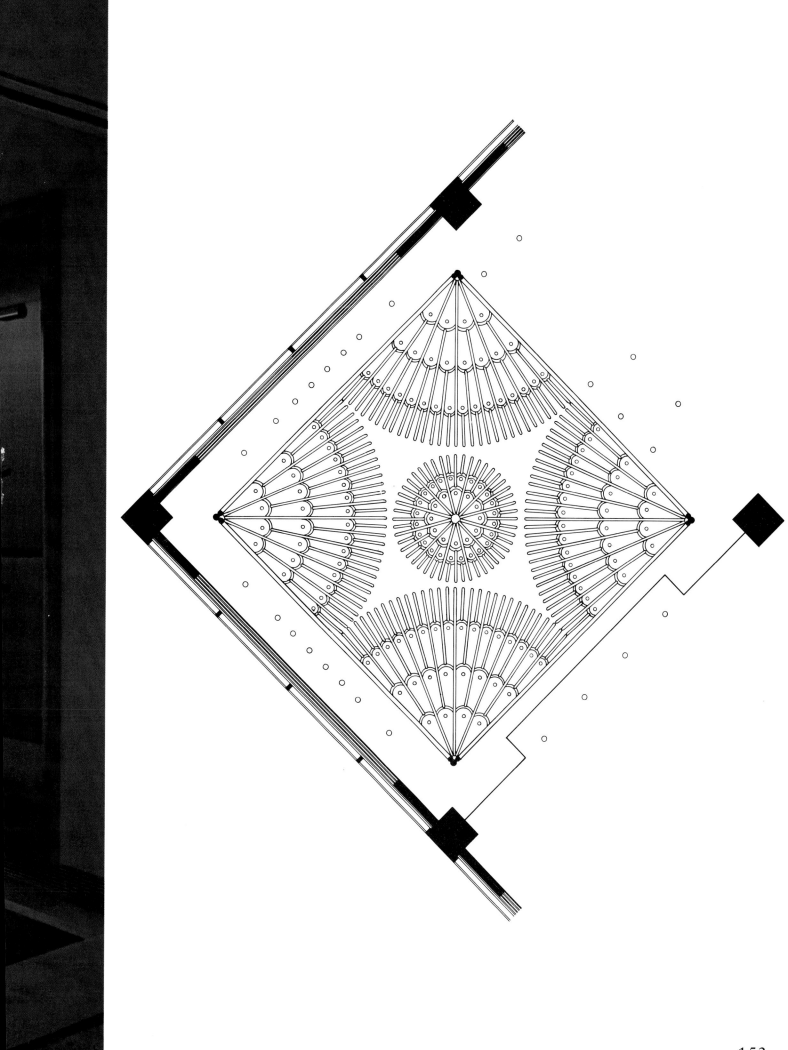

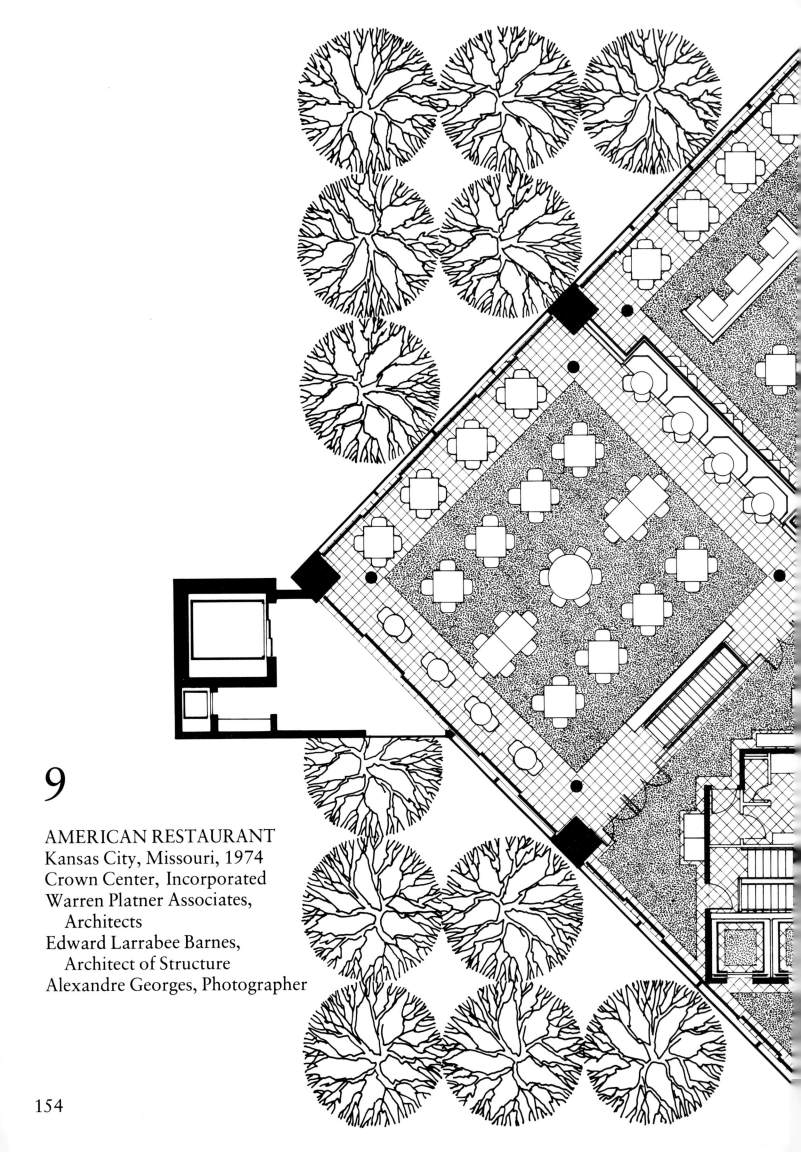

9

AMERICAN RESTAURANT
Kansas City, Missouri, 1974
Crown Center, Incorporated
Warren Platner Associates,
    Architects
Edward Larrabee Barnes,
    Architect of Structure
Alexandre Georges, Photographer

155

10

Not only may a building be conceived from the inside outward but interior space may be used to shape exterior space. Streets and courts are made in this way. Indeed, the mere presence of a building in a landscape is an interruption, a modification of nature. A country house, built to partake of the countryside, can be so thought of. But, conversely, one may conceive of the landscape as flowing through the rooms of a house; space, materials, temperature changing while at some distant point wilderness is no longer wilderness because the house is in view.

Thus, Warren Platner's house was conceived as a modifying of nature's landscape. Inside, it is made of distinct, separate spaces, each room formed for its specific purpose. The structures of these spaces embrace exterior space, room-like terraces wall-enclosed by the house, looking in on the house and out on open terraces and lawns. These in turn overlook both the precincts of house and the distant environs of field, forest, river and sky. There is an interaction between all these spaces of the house, that of the nurturing wilderness and the transition of formal park setting between. Not only are terraces interwoven with the parts of the house and the immediate landscape, but they form exterior rooms extending the house, ultimately appearing as a

garden, a room of flowers walled to over one's head with hemlock hedges, and a tennis court stepped between lawn and reflecting pond, enclosed in leafy banks of pachysandra, tree shaded.

From street and entrance drive this house is invisible, hidden behind trees and hedges. One has no comprehensive picture at the entrance, only parts obscured by plantings, the house unfolding itself and its views only when one is inside. Although one eventually overlooks a succession of terraces, lawns, river valley and hills, none of this becomes apparent until one has entered.

Inside, a great variety of spaces are framed in white, geometric volumes punctuated by dramatic window openings. These openings frame near and distant views, some in volumetric frames, one window within another. They also frame much of the internal aspects of the house, forming seats, embracing dining tables, holding small indoor gardens so arranged that entire rooms seem to be tropically green. Double-bayed windows — one bay within another — work like a camera lens, creating a transition from the large space of the room to a smaller, more digestible view of exterior space, framing and emphasizing it with selective dramatic impact. Thus, in the living room, the center window focuses on oaks across the river, this window in turn framed by a larger one which is then framed by the wall of the room. The larger window provides a peripheral panorama of reflecting pond, tidal salt marsh, fields and, finally, the sky. These windows put tremendous importance on the whole view but temper it, as they also shade and temper the light. In this way, inside the house, one is presented with nature entering from all directions, converging views precisely confined and controlled.

This country house of simple New England materials and uncomplicated forms was built to accommodate the personal life-style of one family, living informally in formal spaces. The fact that one dresses casually, eats in the kitchen and occasionally lies on the floor does not preclude a predilection to be surrounded by beauty. Each of these spaces is a spatial entity, a separate experience, not a flowing together although they do step down the hillside in arrested movement linking them together. Because it is all one house, there is a consistency of color, material and character. Many of the rooms are symmetrical, the volumes of space and the planes of form organized in structural formality. Many of the openings are sculptured into deeply recessing frames or niches. In such a composition, proportions are apparent and important, the bold architectural sculpture assertive. On the other hand, the many personal facets of life in a house – for instance, how the light feels, the sense of enclosure – have made even stronger demands, the satisfying of these conditions in a large measure creating the character.

The centers of life in this house are particular to it, the living room a luminous volume high above the river, the dining room a tropical garden, the kitchen a high-ceilinged artist's studio, serving as the entrance. The great space of the living room, embracing a variety of inner life, is tempered by the special character of where one sits. The center of the room is an enclosing sofa – really a room within the room – supported on and surrounded by upholstered benches, cabinets and table, all a nearly continuous construction reinforcing the quiet character of the center. One may sit within, either on the cushions or the floor, or one may slouch or recline, the related levels of these places making conversation easy. The window seat is a step above, rising over the down-river view, complimenting the lowering of the sofa. Chairs and cushions in the great bay window project one out toward nature as on a sheltered balcony while the bay opposite overlooking the main terrace is filled with orange trees branching into the room. Each of these places is purposefully lighted, and the windows carefully shuttered and shaded. The intent is a place cozy for an evening of one or for a comfortable houseful.

In the dining room, one seems to be surrounded by plants, in reality limited to a bay window. Glass arrangement and orientation is such that the plants grow up and into the room rather than away from the viewer, the plants rather than the people in the sunshine. Terrace plantings directly outside the glass, ground and floor being level, extend the impression of interior garden as does the lighting. At night, garden, table setting, buffet, all seem to emanate inner light to illuminate the occasion of dining.

Landscape flowing through the rooms of the house . . .

. . . terraces, interwove

with interior space like open rooms, flow outward, civilizing the landscape.

The living room's deep recesses frame and control converging views . . .

. . . carving out inner spaces. Special seating places; a window seat one step above the room

at night becomes a flower niche, the window shade in the outer bay painted and lighted as if from within,

at the center of the room . . .   169

. . . secure and enclosing sofas. The fireplace is a bronze mirror, the woodpile a sculpture.

In contrast to the living room's great volume the library is a mirrored corridor,
a pause as the house steps down the hillside . . .

. . . a sidelong glance at the terrace, with a construction of books as an architectural detail.

The personal experience of light and enclosure, of shade and openness . . .

178

. . . of wall and not-wall, are powerful influences in the shaping of the house.

. . . an inner garden, filled with soft, diffused sunlight by day, at night, by a luminescence that seems to emanate from the plants, the table setting and silverware. . . .

A country house of simple New England materials, returning the eye to a wilderness modified by man.

10

RESIDENCE
Guilford, Connecticut, 1971
Warren Platner Associates, Architects
Ezra Stoller, Photographer, except pages 160–61, 172–73, 182
Susan McCartney, Photographer, pages 160–61, 182